NATURE SPY

Wright Group

The McGraw-Hill Companies

NATURE SPY

written by SHELLEY ROTNER and KEN KREISLER
photographs by SHELLEY ROTNER

www.WrightGroup.com

Wright Group

Printed in Mexico.

Send all inquiries to:
Wright Group/McGraw-Hill
P.O. Box 812960
Chicago, IL 60681

ISBN 978-0-07-658183-2
MHID 0-07-658183-7

4 5 6 7 8 9 DRN 16 15 14 13 12 11

For Emily, my little nature spy

—S. R.

For Linda, dream a little dream with me

—K.K.

I like to go outside - to look and discover things.

I like to go outside—to look around and discover things.

Let's go take a closer look.

To take a really close look, even closer

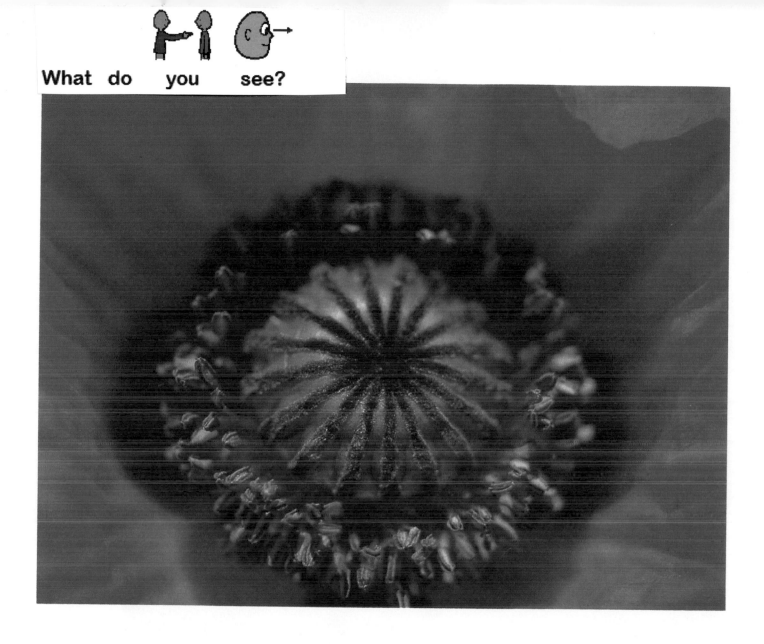

and closer.

I'm a nature spy.

My mother says I'm a curious kid. She calls me a nature spy.

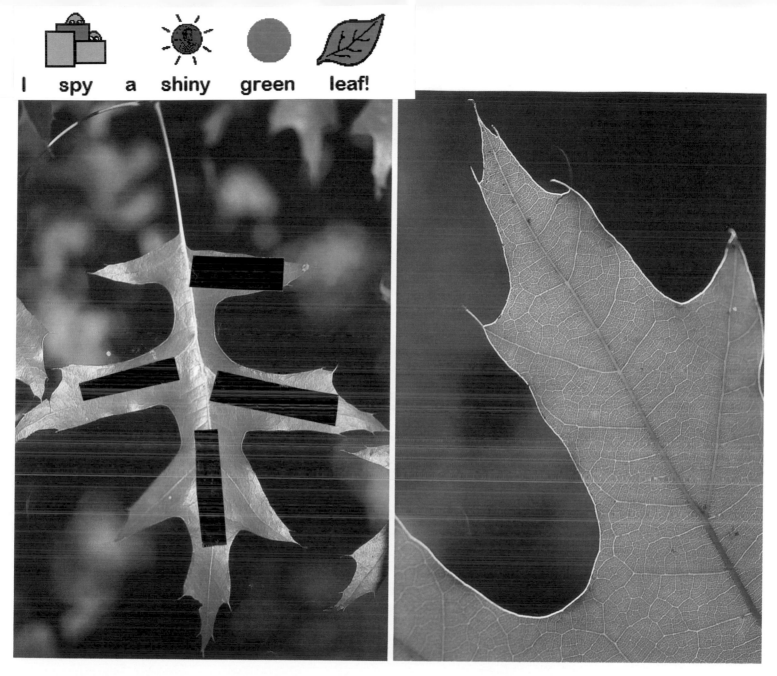

I spy a shiny green leaf!

Sometimes I look so closely, I can see the lines on a shiny green leaf,

I spy a small acorn

or one small acorn on a branch,

and seeds in a pod.

or seeds in a pod.

I spy  feathers on a bird.

I notice the feathers of a bird,

I spy the eye of a frog.

or the golden eye of a frog.

I spy the bark of a tree

When you look closely, things look so different—
like the bark of a tree or an empty hornet's nest,

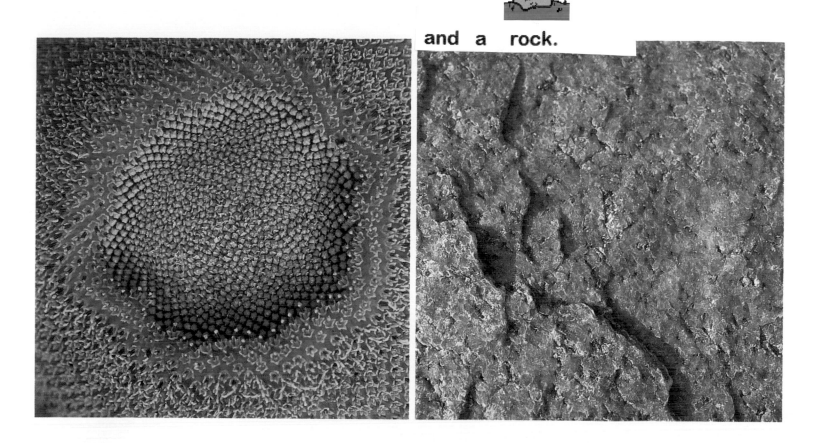

and a rock.

the seeds of a sunflower, or even a rock.

Sometimes there's a pattern, like ice on a frozen pond,

I spy a spiders web and butterfly wings.

or a spider's web, or a butterfly's wing.

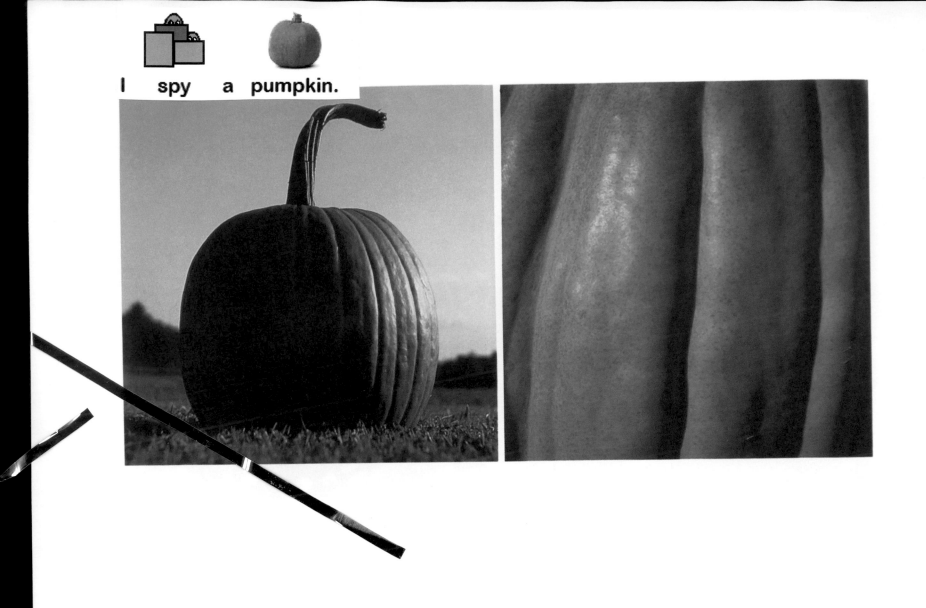

I spy a pumpkin.

Everything has its own shape, color,

and size.

I spy a turtle's shell.

Look closely at a turtle's shell,

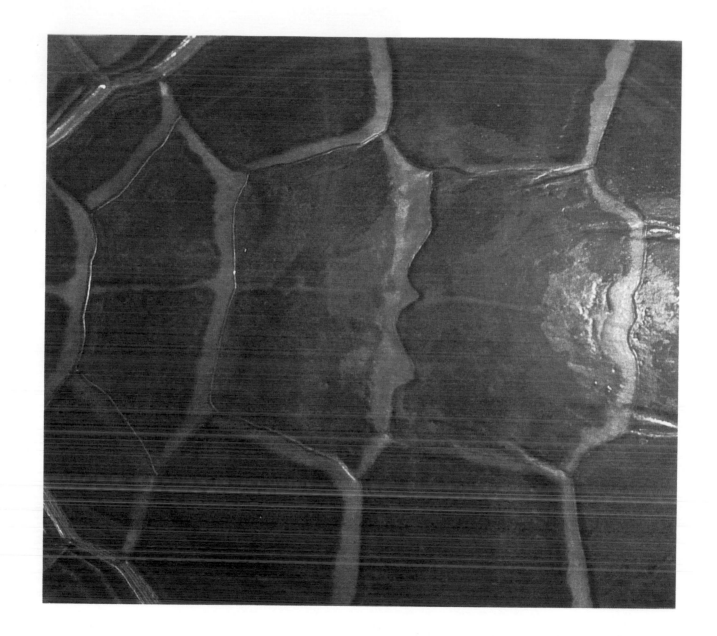

I spy a dog's fur.

or a dog's fur,

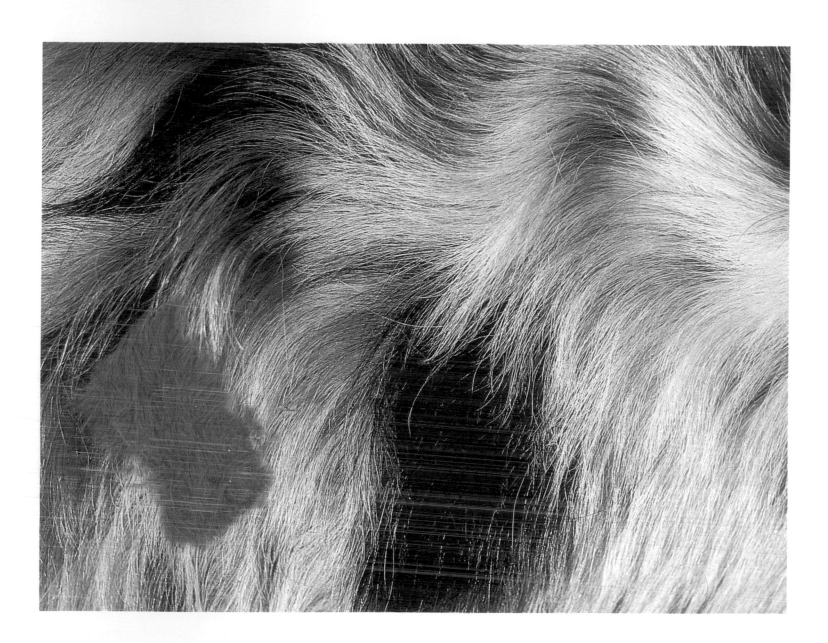

I   spy   raspberries

or even raspberries,

and kernals of corn.

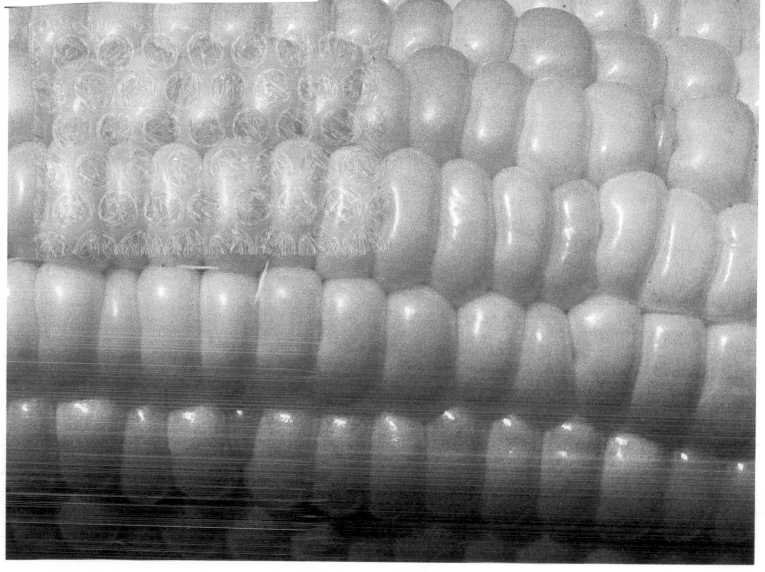

or kernels of corn.

No matter where you look, up, down,

or all around,

There's always something  to see when you're a nature spy!

there's always something to see
when you're a nature spy!